WORDS *of* HOPE *and* HEALING

# IF YOU'RE LONELY
## Finding Your Way

Alan D. Wolfelt, Ph.D.

Companion
**PRESS**

An imprint of the Center for Loss and Life Transition | Fort Collins, Colorado

Companion Press is an imprint of the Center for Loss and Life Transition, 3735 Broken Bow Road, Fort Collins, Colorado 80526.

25  24  23  22  21  20            6  5  4  3  2  1

ISBN: 978-1-61722-297-9

# CONTENTS

# WELCOME

*"The eternal quest of the individual human
being is to shatter his loneliness."*
— Norman Cousins

Loneliness hurts. It may feel like a twinge, a yearning, or an emptiness. It might be more pronounced at certain times than others, or it may be a constant dull ache.

Human beings are social creatures. While each of us is a capable, autonomous individual, we are not meant to exist for very long individually. Since time began, we've lived in social groups. We are built to interact with and rely on others. As a species, we developed highly complex languages—spoken and written—for the purpose of communicating with one another. We divvy up tasks and specialized skills among us because we appreciate that living well is a community effort.

Neurologically, we are also constructed to understand each other's emotions. We have mirror neurons in our brains that fire not only when we ourselves have a certain experience but also when we witness or hear about someone else having that same experience. We are built for empathy, connection, and love.

If you have been feeling lonely, whether all of the time or some of the time, this book is for you. It's possible to find your way out of loneliness. You are a worthy person who needs and deserves connection.

# LONELINESS TODAY

*"To connect to others is a biological need. It ties back to the idea that to be a part of a group is adaptive to survival."*

— Aspen Ideas

One of the great ironies of human life today is that even though there are more of us on this earth than ever, and even though technology has theoretically given us more ways to be connected with one another than ever, many of us have never felt more alone.

We are in the midst of a loneliness epidemic. It's a crisis that cuts across cultures, continents, and classes. Britain has added a Minister for Loneliness to its federal government. In the United States, thirty-five percent of adults over the age of forty-five report feeling lonely. In one recent Cigna survey, over half of Americans said they always or sometimes feel that no one knows them well. And young people are lonely, too. Some studies have found that Millennials and Generation Z are the loneliest of all.

That's the grand scale of the problem. The intimate, personal scale of the problem is the one you may be all too familiar with. That's what we're here to talk about: your loneliness, and what you can do about it.

## WHAT IS LONELINESS?

Loneliness is the feeling of being empty, alone, and unwanted. It's the discomfort or pain of wanting connection with other human beings but not having it. It's an internal response to an external experience (or lack thereof).

We'll tease apart the various facets of loneliness in a bit, but for now I'll just say that from the outside looking in, loneliness is often invisible and undetectable. Not everyone who is lonely is alone. Some lonely people live in chockfull apartment buildings in New York City. Some lonely people work in offices or places with dozens or hundreds of coworkers. And some lonely people seem to have full lives and many friends.

The bottom line is that if you feel lonely, you are lonely. And there are ways to break through your particular loneliness, no matter its causes or qualities. There is hope, and there is help. Though you feel lonely, you are not alone.

## THE STIGMA OF LONELINESS

Have you felt ashamed or embarrassed of your loneliness? This is common because as a culture we tend to associate loneliness with a failure of interpersonal skills, a lack of strength, or a weakness of character. This unfair and inaccurate stigma can get compounded by ageism. When older people are lonely (and they are, in staggering numbers), it tends to be an unseemly topic that we don't want to examine or talk about.

But you and I are here to talk about it. In our world today, loneliness is a normal human response to isolation. It's largely caused by the structure of modern society—not by the actions, inactions, or inherent qualities of individuals like you. In other words, it's not your fault. Loneliness is not a personal failing or character flaw.

I hope this book will help you grow more comfortable with acknowledging and understanding your loneliness as well as expressing and easing it. We have to get better at talking about uncomfortable feelings. Only through honest awareness and open discussion can we find ways to create a healthier, connected culture.

WHY ARE SO MANY PEOPLE TODAY LONELY?

Loneliness rates have doubled in the United States in the past fifty years. Why?

One reason is that people used to live in households comprised of multiple generations, sometimes with grandparents, parents, aunts and uncles, and children all living together. Today generations are separated into their own households (though in recent years this trend is starting to reverse somewhat). Nearly a third of American seniors age sixty-five or older live alone—double the percentage of most other countries. In addition, marriage is becoming less common, and couples are having fewer children—or no children at all.

Rising isolation in the home has taken hold concurrent with the rise in technology. In lieu of face-to-face conversation, we now rely on email and texts to communicate with one another. And instead of visiting local shops, restaurants, and banks, we now order online, have our goods and food delivered, and swap digital currency.

Social media is part of this technology tsunami, of course. Facebook, Instagram, Twitter, and other digital social networks are taking the place of the downtown evening stroll, the Saturday night dance, and the community potluck. And while they're highly effective at some things, such as quickly sharing news and uniting people who are physically distant, social media platforms are sorely lacking in physical presence, facial expressions, tone of voice, and personal warmth.

Workplaces, too, used to be more interactive. Before everyone became glued to computer screens, people worked more closely with one another. Think of the old country doctor versus today's general practitioner, who is forced to gaze into her laptop more than into the eyes of her patients. Or consider the grocery store, where self-checkout is fast replacing human checkers. Or the technology industry itself, which is now divesting itself of workplaces altogether and instead dispersing many employees to work remotely in their own homes.

Here in America, we are also infected by the "ideal" of rugged individualism. Coined by Herbert Hoover in 1928, this term encapsulated the misguided notion that individuals should be self-reliant and independent, not counting on others for support. And long before that, woven into the very foundation of our country, was the Puritan belief in self-restraint and stoicism. The trouble is, if you keep your emotions to yourself and believe it's wrong to rely on others, loneliness is a natural byproduct.

The societal causes of the loneliness epidemic will not be quickly remedied. For now what we can do is work to understand them and support policy and process changes that move us in the direction of meaningful connectedness and mutual reliance. On a personal level, though, there are many things we can do to help with our loneliness. We'll be talking about those soon.

## SITUATIONS THAT GIVE RISE TO LONELINESS

People can be lonely at any time for myriad reasons, but these are some of the common circumstances that lead to loneliness:

- Death of a partner
- Divorce from a partner
- Single parenting
- Separation or estrangement from loved ones
- Empty nest
- Work addiction, unemployment, starting a new job, or retirement
- Poor health, especially if you have become housebound or have mobility issues
- Being the primary caregiver at home for an elderly or ill person
- Technology addiction
- Relocation to a new city, state, or country
- Normal aging, leading to living alone and diminished capacity to interact
- Isolation due to personal differences

I'm sure you can think of more causes of loneliness. Why are you lonely? Whatever your reasons, they belong on this list as well.

## LONELINESS AFTER A DEATH

As you can imagine, as a grief counselor and educator I have often supported people struggling with loneliness after the death of someone significant in their life. Loneliness and sadness are indeed two hallmark symptoms of grief after the death of a loved one. Loneliness is often especially prominent when the person who died was a daily companion or routine presence in the life of the person who is grieving.

If someone you were sharing your life with has died, it's normal to feel lonely. Loneliness is a necessary part of your grief, but like other emotions you are experiencing, it is painful and difficult. If the person who died was your partner or longtime companion, this may be the first time in your life you've been forced to encounter profound loneliness, making it extra difficult.

I want you to know that you can and will get through this. Your life will never be the same, but by following the principles in this book, you can find your way to new meaning, purpose, and connection. In fact, many mourners have taught me that through active mourning, self-care, and reaching out to others, over time they have discovered surprising new joys and fulfillment. You can too. You deserve connection and contentment. I hope you will believe in yourself as much as I believe in you.

## WHY IS LONELINESS SO BAD FOR US?

As we said, loneliness hurts. That alone makes loneliness a significant mental health issue that merits attention. But not only does loneliness wound us emotionally, it causes measurable physical harm. Studies show that lonely people are more likely to get sick, suffer cognitive decline, and die sooner. Scientists have learned that loneliness even affects the body on the cellular level. Social isolation can trigger chronic inflammation, which heightens the risk of heart disease, stroke, cancer, and dementia.

Loneliness is a personal mental wellness challenge, but it's also a public health threat as ominous as any pandemic or global climate danger.

## MEASURING YOUR LONELINESS

There's something called the UCLA Loneliness Scale that attempts to help doctors, therapists, and other caregivers measure the severity of people's loneliness. I've come up with my own questionnaire here to help you take a closer look at your loneliness and identify possible areas of focus to begin to ease it.

| THE WOLFELT LONELINESS INVENTORY<br>Next to each statement, circle the number that fits best. | Never | Rarely | Sometimes | Often |
|---|---|---|---|---|
| I see other people in stores and places I visit routinely. | 1 | 2 | 3 | 4 |
| I am around other people in my daily life. | 1 | 2 | 3 | 4 |
| I chat a bit with strangers in public places. | 1 | 2 | 3 | 4 |
| **PROXIMITY SCORE** (out of 12) | | | | |
| | | | | |
| I know my neighbors and talk to them. | 1 | 2 | 3 | 4 |
| I feel part of several communities. | 1 | 2 | 3 | 4 |
| I participate in groups and share the same interests as other people I socialize with. | 1 | 2 | 3 | 4 |
| I feel connected to my community. | 1 | 2 | 3 | 4 |
| **COMMUNITY SCORE** (out of 16) | | | | |
| | | | | |
| I feel that I have companionship in my daily life. | 1 | 2 | 3 | 4 |
| I feel that I have meaningful relationships with people I care about. | 1 | 2 | 3 | 4 |
| I have people in my life to spend holidays and other special days with. | 1 | 2 | 3 | 4 |

*Continued on next page...*

| THE WOLFELT LONELINESS INVENTORY (CONTINUED) | Never | Rarely | Sometimes | Often |
|---|---|---|---|---|
| I feel other people know me pretty well. | 1 | 2 | 3 | 4 |
| **CLOSE COMMUNITY SCORE** (out of 16) | | | | |
| I feel like I have people I can talk to about my biggest dreams, worries, and losses. | 1 | 2 | 3 | 4 |
| I have the amount of physical closeness or touch in my life that I want. | 1 | 2 | 3 | 4 |
| I have the amount of sex in my life that I want. | 1 | 2 | 3 | 4 |
| I feel I have the best friend(s) I want. | 1 | 2 | 3 | 4 |
| I feel I have the partner I want. | 1 | 2 | 3 | 4 |
| **INTIMATE RELATIONSHIPS SCORE** (out of 20) | | | | |
| I feel good about myself. | 1 | 2 | 3 | 4 |
| I treat myself with kindness and self-compassion. | 1 | 2 | 3 | 4 |
| I take good care of myself. | 1 | 2 | 3 | 4 |
| **SELF-RELATIONSHIP SCORE** (out of 12) | | | | |
| **TOTAL SCORE** (out of 76) | | | | |

**Correction**

The Wolfelt Loneliness Inventory score key printed on page 13 is incorrect. It should say:

| | |
|---|---|
| 19-38 | severe loneliness |
| 39-57 | moderate loneliness |
| 58-76 | mild loneliness |

We apologize for the error. It will be corrected in the second printing of this book.

Before we talk about loneliness scores, I want to emphasize that loneliness is not truly a measurable experience. The scale I've created is meant only to help you begin to understand your loneliness better. If you feel deeply lonely, you are deeply lonely, no matter what your score may say. The same goes for minimal or more occasional loneliness. With those caveats firmly in mind, on this scale, 19-38 points to mild loneliness, 39-57 moderate loneliness, and 58-76 severe loneliness. In addition to understanding the degree of your loneliness, the sections in the scale will also help you discern which areas of your life would most benefit from more connection.

## MOURNING YOUR LONELINESS

Now that you've taken the measure of your loneliness (again, keeping in mind that this scoring system is an imperfect tool), I want to take a moment to acknowledge your sorrow. I have been a grief counselor for forty years, so I understand that loneliness is a form of loss. For one, your loneliness may have come to you on the heels of great loss in your life. If people close to you have died or left, for example, or if you retired from a job where you had good friends and colleagues, you are likely to miss them and experience loneliness. And for another, the lack of love and connection in life is itself a kind of loss. When your expectations, hopes, and dreams for your life don't come to pass, the gap between what you wanted and the reality you are living also naturally gives rise to grief.

Your grief over the circumstances that have caused your loneliness is normal and necessary. You have every right to feel sad, angry, rejected, or however you feel. And expressing—or mourning—that grief is an essential part of self-care.

I encourage you to talk to someone about your loneliness, perhaps a counselor or a clergyperson. I also encourage you to try other ways of expressing your loneliness. You might write in a journal, participate in a support group, join an online forum, or create art. The more you express your grief over your loneliness, the better able you will be to acknowledge it, understand it, and find your way through it.

### A CALL TO ACTION

Loneliness tends to breed more loneliness. Studies have shown that people who feel lonely are likely to lose more connections over time because fewer interactions with existing acquaintances leads to fewer interactions with new acquaintances, and so on. Loneliness is often a progressive problem, so it's helpful to catch it as early as possible, and it's important to take action to address it as soon as possible.

If you're suffering from loneliness, you deserve to feel better.

If You're Lonely

You deserve a full life, and that includes a variety of kinds of human connection. What's more, it is within your power to take steps to begin to ease your loneliness. In other words, you can learn to be proactive about countering your loneliness. That's one of the funny things about loneliness, actually—you may think you need others to come to you, but the truth is that you yourself can bridge the gap.

If you are severely lonely right now, especially if you think you might be clinically depressed and definitely if you have had thoughts of suicide, I urge you to talk to your primary healthcare provider as well as a therapist right away. They can help you through this immediate period of crisis, and the ideas in this book will support you in the longer term. Again, there is help, and there is hope.

# MAKING FRIENDS
# WITH YOURSELF

*"When we love, we always strive to become better than we are.
When we strive to become better than we are, everything around us
becomes better, too."*

— Paulo Coelho

In many ways, combating loneliness starts with your own feelings about yourself. Being your own best friend is a strong foundation for good mental health in general. But—perhaps counterintuitively—it's also essential to effective relationships with other people. In other words, solid self-awareness, self-esteem, self-advocacy, and self-care create a "you" that is prepared to interact well with others.

Do you have a hard time believing in yourself? Did your upbringing make you feel bad about yourself in any way? Do you have trouble sticking up for your own beliefs, values, and needs? Do you sometimes seem overly needy or volatile to others? Do you tend to take poor care of yourself? If you answered yes to any of these questions, now is a good time to focus on befriending yourself on the path to more connection with others.

Of course, I'm not advocating for egotism or narcissism. People who are wholly wrapped up in themselves aren't capable of empathizing with and caring about others. (Maybe you know folks like this?) Instead, what I'm recommending here is authentic self-compassion and self-respect. If you don't love, value, and care for yourself, it's much harder for others to love, value, and care for you.

Yet I also recognize that loneliness and low self-esteem often go hand-in-hand. It can become a vicious cycle. If you feel inadequate, you're less likely to have the confidence to "put yourself out there" and establish relationships. And so you become lonely, and your self-esteem falls further…and so on and so on. If you believe your loneliness may be tied to chronic low self-esteem, I hope you will both work actively on cultivating self-compassion and developing good-self-care *and* start seeing a counselor. Getting to the root of poor self-esteem and finding effective ways to rebuild it is absolutely possible, but it's also challenging work. A trained professional will help you be successful in this lifesaving quest.

## CARING FOR YOURSELF PHYSICALLY, EMOTIONALLY, COGNITIVELY, SOCIALLY, AND SPIRITUALLY

As you consider whether or not you're already good friends with yourself, I want you to think about all the ways you care for yourself—and fail to take care of yourself—right now. You have physical, emotional, cognitive, social, and spiritual needs. We'll be talking a lot more about social needs in the pages to come, so let's set that one aside for the moment.

First, good physical self-care is a nonnegotiable part of self-love. The right amount of high-quality sleep is necessary; no one functions well in life without it. Adequate daily exercise, decent nutrition, and good hydration (with water!) are also necessary.

Second, emotional self-care requires that you foster awareness of your own thoughts and feelings and express them appropriately. Emotional intelligence is the capacity to be aware of, control, and express your emotions to others. High "EQ" allows you to communicate well with others and handle relationships effectively. To build your EQ, work on being aware of what you are feeling in the moment, responding calmly to conflict, and honing your active listening and empathy skills.

Third, cognitive self-care involves being aware of your

thoughts, challenging and correcting any habitual negative thinking, affirming personal strengths, and engaging in activities that feed and develop your brain, such as reading and learning new things. Meditation is a wonderful cognitive self-care tool. It teaches you to calm your mind and find your center, which in turn helps you bring your kind presence to others.

And finally, spiritual self-care recognizes that you are a spiritual being who desires meaning and purpose in this life. Whatever helps you contemplate the meaning of your life or feel a powerful sense of satisfaction and "rightness"—do that. Some people pray. Others volunteer. Still others read spiritual texts, attend services or workshops, meditate, do yoga, or spend time in nature.

As you think about the goals of self-care, please understand that I am not asking you to be perfect! You deserve self-love and connection with others no matter what, just by virtue of being a miraculous, singular human being. Rather, what I hope to impress upon you is that actively working on self-awareness and self-care is a necessary part of finding your way past loneliness.

For now, consider picking just one self-care activity to focus on. The wonderful thing is that self-care tends to snowball. If you start by going for a short walk every day, for example, you'll begin to feel stronger and more capable of taking part in other physical activities. Your brain will get better blood flow, leading to enhanced learning and thinking. Your emotions, fed by those happy brain chemicals, will become more joyful and hopeful. You'll be more capable of connecting well with others and finding shared interests. All because you launched the simple habit of taking a daily walk.

## ISOLATION VERSUS SOLITUDE

Loneliness is a feeling of isolation and apartness from others. As we've already affirmed, you can feel lonely whether you're with others or actually physically alone. So isolation can be an external physical reality, an internal feeling, or both.

Solitude, on the other hand, is being alone without feeling lonely. On the contrary, solitude can be a sought-after oasis that allows you to reflect, get in touch with your spirit, and grow emotionally and spiritually.

As you work on self-awareness and self-care, you may find that some of your feelings of isolation may transform into appreciation for solitude. Essentially, the more you befriend yourself, the more appreciative you may become of the joys of being alone some of the time.

## THINGS TO DO TO FEEL LESS LONELY

- Call or text a friend
- Cuddle with a pet
- Get lost in a favorite book or movie
- Help someone else in some small way—anonymously
- Go for a walk, and pick up trash as you go
- Do something creative
- Look through old photos and reminisce
- Make plans to visit a friend, attend an event, or participate in a gathering
- Play your favorite music and sing or dance along
- Be generous in some way
- Start a gratitude journal
- Meditate
- Engage with social media, but only if it makes you feel good
- Take a bath and pamper yourself
- Pop into a coffee shop
- Take photos of the people and places in your neighborhood
- Try something you've always wanted to try
- Bake cookies and share them with others
- Go for a drive or bike ride
- Practice random acts of kindness

## WIELDING VULNERABILITY

Sometimes loneliness is caused or heightened by an unwillingness to be vulnerable.

In our emotional toolkits, vulnerability is a powerful instrument. As Brené Brown says, "Vulnerability is the birthplace of innovation, creativity, and change." I would add that it's the also the birthplace of connection with others.

When we extend ourselves to other people, offering up all the authentic qualities that make us, us, we are saying, "Here I am. Look at me. I'm worthy of being in your life." That's a vulnerable place to be because those people might reject us. They have the power to welcome us in, to ignore us, or to rebuff us altogether.

But to be vulnerable is to take risks to reach for what we want in life. There is no other way to get where we want to go. And even though we sometimes make mistakes and things don't always unfold as we wish they would, the rewards of wielding vulnerability are ultimately so much greater than the deadening missed opportunities of playing it safe.

To reiterate: Loneliness comes from avoiding emotional risk. Connection comes from allowing and then actively wielding vulnerability.

So as you work on befriending yourself, I want you to remember that it's good to be vulnerable. It's necessary to put yourself out there. You're lonely, and finding your way through loneliness to connection requires you take some chances and learn to wield vulnerability like the scepter it is. What do you really have to lose?

### CREATING A VISION AND SETTING YOUR INTENTION

Before we begin to discuss building connections with others, I'd like you to stop and consider what your life would look like if you were no longer lonely. Each of us has our own unique dreams and desires for connection and ideas about what constitutes a happy life. So it's important for you to be clear about what *you* want.

What do you envision for your unlonely future? How would your days be different than they are now? What will have been added to your life, and what will have been subtracted?

Please take a moment to envision the future you desire. Jot down your ideas here.

---

---

---

---

---

_____

_____

_____

_____

_____

_____

_____

_____

_____

_____

_____

Now set your intention to move toward this desired future.

I have been lonely because _____

_____

_____

_____

_____

_____

_____

_____

_____

_____

_____.

I have envisioned the changed life I want to lead instead. I
commit to moving toward this desired future through self-
awareness, self-care, and building connections with others.

# BUILDING CONNECTIONS WITH OTHERS

*"Keep in mind that to avoid loneliness, many people
need both a social circle and an intimate attachment.
Having just one of two may still leave you feeling lonely."*

— Gretchen Rubin

Finding your way past loneliness involves befriending yourself and befriending others. But as you have probably realized, it's not as simple as saying, "I just need to make friends" or "I just need to socialize more."

For one, making friends and socializing is difficult for some people, and the more disconnected you are at this point, the more difficult it can be. For another, you may already have friends and social circles yet still feel lonely. So, understanding the source and unique qualities of your particular loneliness will help you make a good plan to find your way through.

## CIRCLES OF CONNECTION

All of us are part of a number of communities and relationships. And all of these together form our circles of connection.

Depending on your life circumstances right now, you may be connected to your immediate family (partner and children, if you have them), your chosen family (close friends),

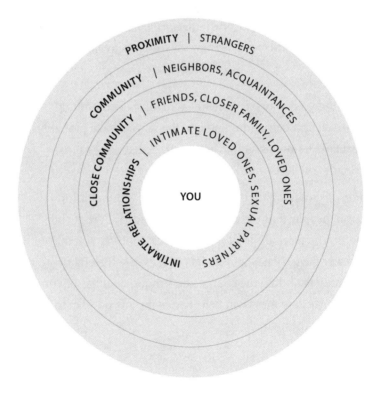

your family of origin (mother, father, siblings), your casual friends and acquaintances, your extended family, your work community, your neighborhood, any groups or organizations you belong to, and the city or town in which you live.

In the Wolfelt Loneliness Inventory on page 11, you scored your sense of loneliness in several circles: proximity, community, close community, intimate relationships, and you. Any section with a low score (mostly 1s and 2s) is an area in your circles of connection that would probably benefit from strengthening and maybe expanding.

Yet keep in mind that each person's need for connection is different. Based on your personality, degree of extroversion or introversion (see pg. 32), and life circumstances, you may feel well connected with lots of people in your life or just a few. In general, I would say that it's necessary to have a tribe. That is, it's important to have connections in all of the concentric circles, even if you only have one or two solid entries in each circle. In addition, when it comes to combating loneliness, the most important circles are those toward the center. If your relationships with yourself, intimate others, and close community are strong and fulfilling, you are less likely to feel lonely.

But even at the periphery of the overall circle, connection helps dissolve loneliness. Studies have shown that people who interact and chat with strangers are less lonely. It turns out that having a brief small-talk exchange with your barista or your neighbor walking his dog can make a big difference. Even simple eye contact with strangers has been proven to boost people's mood and increase their sense of belonging. To see and be seen by another human being is affirming.

And don't overlook the fact that "you" are in the center of the circles of connection. That's the oh-so-important self-esteem/self-care work we talked about in the last chapter, and it's why I discussed making friends with yourself before diving into the topic of social self-care and building connections with others. In fact, excellent self-esteem and self-care ripple out from the center, naturally engaging and buoying all of the other circles. Conversely, poor self-esteem and self-care ripple out from the center but have the opposite effect. They damage and weaken the connections in all of the other circles. Think of healthy self-love as propelling good vibes through the circles of connection and poor self-love as emanating weak and sometimes even toxic vibes.

## TAKING STOCK OF YOUR EXISTING CONNECTIONS
Now let's take a look at the circles of connection again and note where you might benefit from better connection. I invite you to note your loneliness scores from page 11 in the designated spots as well as jot down a few thoughts about

Proximity Score:

Community Score:

Close Community Score:

Intimate Relationships Score:

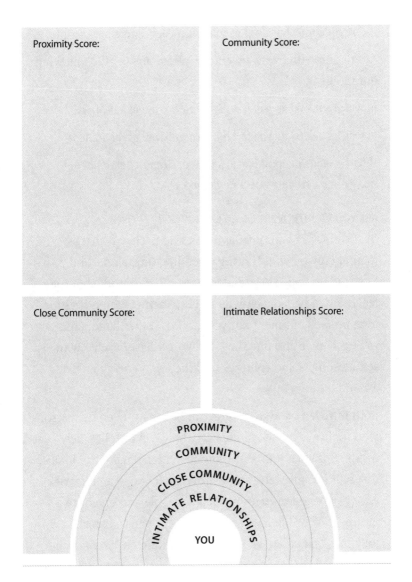

PROXIMITY

COMMUNITY

CLOSE COMMUNITY

INTIMATE RELATIONSHIPS

YOU

the people and habits that make up each circle in your life.

After completing your inventory, please answer the following questions:

*In which circle(s) do you feel the greatest sense of loneliness?*

*In which circle(s) do you feel the greatest sense of connection?*

*Where would you most like to focus your connection-building energy in the coming weeks and months?*

### ARE YOU AN INTROVERT OR AN EXTROVERT?

Introverts are often quiet and observant. They recharge their energy by withdrawing, spending time alone, and focusing inward. They tend to be good at solitude, but they feel drained by large crowds and interacting with others for long periods of time. Extroverts, on the other hand, tend to be talkative and outgoing. They may have trouble with self-awareness and solitude, and they gain energy by being around other people.

Both introverts and extroverts can be lonely. Even the person who is always the life of the party may feel deeply lonely inside. But what it takes to counteract loneliness may look different for introverts and extroverts. If you're an introvert, strong connections with just a few people and one or two groups in your life may be sufficient for you to banish loneliness. If you're an extrovert, working on "you"—self-awareness and self-love—may be a good area of focus. You may also need to work on building stronger, deeper, more vulnerable relationships with those you are closest to.

## PROXIMITY, REPETITION, AND QUALITY TIME

How do you build strong bonds with others? Through proximity, repetition, and quality time.

This may sound totally obvious, but when we're physically near someone frequently, we're more likely to develop a strong relationship with them. Being together in person is best, but when that's not possible—such as when people live in different communities, for example—it's still possible to maintain close ties through frequent video calls, emails, and texts.

But quality time is the other essential factor here. As you may have experienced yourself, you can be around someone every day yet not feel close to them. Perhaps you even live in the same household with others yet feel like you don't have effective, cherished relationships with them.

Emotional bonds are built on quality time. What does that mean? Quality time is time spent with another person or people in which you are focusing on each other, communicating well, and empathizing. You can be in the same room with another person, each immersed in your own phone. This is not quality time. But if you sit together in front of the same laptop or a TV, watching a favorite show and chatting about it as it plays, that may count as quality time. Similarly, distractedly talking "at" each other while you're busy with other things is not quality time, but stopping to look each other in the eyes and really give one another undivided attention—that's the quality time that's needed to build love and devotion.

Stop for a second and think about the most cherished moments in your life—the ones that not only bring a smile to your face but also tug at your heart. It's likely they were spent sharing quality time with those you loved the most. That's one of the most important questions I hope you will keep in mind as you find your way through loneliness: How can I spend more quality time with people I care about?

Now let's talk about building connection in each of the concentric circles, from the inside out. We've already talked about befriending yourself, so we'll start with intimate relationships.

### BUILDING INTIMATE RELATIONSHIPS

For many people, loving intimate relationships are central to feeling a sense of connection and well-being in life.

Intimacy is close familiarity. When you are intimate with someone, it means you know them well and they know you well. Loving intimacy means that you have strong bonds formed by proximity, repetition, and quality time. Physical touch and sex can also be essential parts of intimacy, but for most people they are secondary to emotional closeness.

Life partners and best friends are the relationships in this circle of connection. If your loneliness stems in part from a lack of a partner and/or best friends, this will be an important area for you to focus on. You may desire a partner *and* best friends, or you might want the companionship of best friends only.

In addition, I would be remiss if I failed to address here the fact that many lonely people *do* have partners and close friends yet don't find these relationships meaningful enough. In the Wolfelt Loneliness Inventory, I asked if you have the partner and best friend(s) you *want*. That's because you can live in the same household with a partner with whom you're not a close companion or a fulfilled, intimate significant other. Likewise, you can have longtime best friends whom you've grown apart from, who don't share your interests or passions, or who aren't capable of providing you with the mutual trust, acknowledgment, and companionship you desire. For purposes of this discussion, having no partner or best-friend relationship is the same as technically having those relationships yet finding them unmeaningful. Ditto for close community and community in the circles of connection.

If you are looking for a new partner, I urge you to focus on self-love as much as you do on your search for a partner. You will find that the self-love practices naturally create opportunities for close connections with others to develop. I also urge you to work on strengthening the friendships you already have, because friendships that grow into partnerships are often among the strongest and longest-lasting partnerships there are.

Online dating services are a common partner-finding tool today, of course, and they do work for some people. Thirty percent of Americans have used them. Networking with friends to meet their friends is another good way. Remember the call to wield vulnerability? Using dating sites and getting set up on blind dates is a way to do this. But I think possibly the best avenue for finding a potential partner is pursuing your own interests in ways that bring you into contact with other people.

If you get involved in organizations you support, volunteer for causes that matter to you, and take part in activities you enjoy, you will naturally meet people with whom you have meaningful things in common. Remember proximity, repetition, and quality time. The more you commit yourself to being near people frequently and spending quality time together, the more likely you are to develop close friendships and, if you're looking for intimate love, a partnership.

## OFFLOADING BUSYNESS, JAMPACKING MEANING

Some very busy people are lonely. Their days may be full, but their hearts are empty.

If you feel lonely despite being busy or overscheduled, consider what gives you a sense of meaning and purpose. Which people and activities deplete you, and which fill you up? It's time to eliminate as many of the former as possible and jampack your life with the latter.

It's also possible that some of your sense of loneliness stems from an imbalance of time. If you had more time to focus on the circles of meaningful connection you already have in your life, do you think your loneliness might ease of its own accord? If so, this is may be a critical area of focus for you.

## BUILDING CLOSE COMMUNITY

For many people who are lonely, transforming acquaintances and loose family ties into friends and loved ones is an ideal place to start proactively working on banishing loneliness.

It's likely that you have some acquaintances and/or loose family ties. How can you grow closer to some of these people? Again, the answer lies in proximity, repetition, and quality time.

It's typically most effective to work on building relationships with people who live nearby. That doesn't mean you can't and shouldn't build relationships with people who are far away—only that long-distance relationships typically won't significantly ease your day-to-day loneliness. So consider acquaintances and family members you like or used to be close to who live in your neighborhood or city. Reach out to them and invite them over or out to lunch. Or ask them to accompany you to some event or activity. Offering to help them in some way can be another good connection builder. As long as the get-together allows you to talk with and get to know each other better, it counts as quality time.

That covers proximity and quality time. What about repetition? Building relationships requires *frequent* contact. How frequent depends on what's appropriate and mutually pleasing to the other individual. Some people will feel bothered by too-frequent contact, while others will feel abandoned if you're not in touch often enough (for them). There's no one right way. There is only continually doing the work of being a steady presence in someone else's life.

And if you need more prospects for building close community, pursuing your own interests in ways that bring you into contact with other people is again your best bet. If you're a reader, join a book club. If you're a fisherman, volunteer for an organization that supports habitat restoration or teaches others how to fish. If you're a spiritual seeker, join a worship or meditation community. Find ways to be near people with whom you have mutual interests. And when you have the opportunity to be vulnerable, do so. Ask a new acquaintance more about themselves, or express interest in their lives in some way. Share a bit about yourself, too. This is how friendships are built and deepened.

## THE "MUTUAL" IN RELATIONSHIPS

As you work to build relationships in your life, remember that to be satisfying to both parties, relationships must be a two-way street. You are in need of others, and they must also be in need of you. It can be tricky to figure out what each person wants out of a relationship, how much time each likes to spend together, how to communicate effectively, etc. Everyone, including those who are well connected and not lonely, is challenged by these relationship dynamics.

My advice to you is don't give up. Work on your EQ and persist in trying to find that sweet spot of mutual satisfaction with friends and partners. Relationships of all kinds require ongoing TLC. It can be hard work, but ultimately it's the most satisfying work in life.

## BUILDING COMMUNITY

In your circles of connection, this is the realm of neighbors and casual acquaintances. You build this level of connection by making yourself known to these people and by opening the door to closer friendships.

Do you know your neighbors' names, and do they know yours? If not, this is a good place to start. After names comes sharing a little basic information about each other. To help banish loneliness and strengthen your circles of connection, you don't need to become good friends with people in this circle, although you might. What you need—and what they need, too—is a sense of belonging to a community of people who are looking out for each other.

Neighbors have proximity and repetition to work with, of course. What about casual acquaintances? How do you stay connected to them? When you meet someone new, it may not be appropriate or desirable for you to be in touch with them after that, but you can work to remember their name and interests. Then, when you stumble upon something that might be of interest to them in the future, you may be able to let them know, shoring up your connection. Or at the very least you can strike up a meaningful conversation if you happen to run into them again.

When it comes to this general community level in your circles of connection, I urge you to simply remember that people matter. You matter and deserve connection and love. That's why I'm writing this book. But all of the people you meet in life deserve connection and love, too. You can and should be someone who offers that to them. You do this by making eye contact, saying hello, remembering their name, honoring the divine in them, and when you're in conversation, expressing a genuine interest in their lives and whatever is important to them.

## THE POWER OF NAMASTE

In the US, the Sanskrit word "namaste" is often used at the close of yoga classes. Participants press their palms together in front of their chest and in unison say namaste, which loosely means "the divine in me honors the divine in you."

The concept of namaste recognizes that each individual person we encounter is special and worthy of acknowledgment. As you work to build community, it might be useful to remember this idea. Looking strangers in the eye and greeting them with a friendly smile and a few kind words, when appropriate, is in the spirit of namaste. Not only will this simple practice help you feel more connected to others, it will remind you that you, too, are worthy of everyday acknowledgment and kindness.

### BUILDING PROXIMITY

To build proximity in your circles of connection is simply to take advantage of opportunities to be around other people often if you're not already.

As we've discussed, isolation is harmful both psychologically and physically. Simply being in the presence of other people—at the grocery store, a coffee shop, worship services, restaurants, libraries, etc.—eases that sense of being alone and disconnected from life. Once you're out and about, leveraging the power of namaste to look strangers in the eye, smile, and say hello can then open up an important additional layer of connection.

If you are largely homebound for any reason, or if you are geographically isolated, building proximity may be especially challenging. I urge you to look into community services that enable mobility and/or connection, such as senior transportation assistance, Meals on Wheels, and respite care if your isolation is due to being the primary caregiver for an ill or elderly loved one. Remember that you need and deserve connection, and there are people and services who want to help. Those who live in remote locations may need to find creative ways to connect with others each week and take advantage of every opportunity to visit loved ones, host houseguests, and join up in rural get-togethers.

### ADDING COMPANION ANIMALS

Many people find deep comfort and companionship in their relationships with their dogs, cats, birds, rabbits, guinea pigs, horses, and other companion animals. Do you have a pet? If so, you probably know well what a source of love and fulfillment they can be.

The benefits of having furry and feathered friends are many. They are always there for us, providing us with constant, loyal companionship. They offer unconditional love and acceptance. They improve our mood. They provide us with daily activities that get us up and moving, such as going for walks, brushing and feeding, and even cleaning up after them. And they also can facilitate our connection with other humans. If you take your dog to the dog park, for example, you're likely to get to know the other dog owners who regularly gather there.

What's more, pets fulfill our human need for touch. Petting and hugging our companion animals, and having them sit on our laps or snuggle up next to us, elevate our happy brain chemicals in the same way that the touch of other people does.

For some people who are lonely, having a close companion animal or two can even partially fill the intimate relationships circle of connection.

Pets aren't for everyone, but it's for good reason that nearly seventy percent of U.S. households share their home with at least one pet. If you don't have a pet right now, I hope you'll consider adopting one that suits your lifestyle, volunteering at an animal shelter, or spending time with one that belongs to a friend or neighbor.

## ADDING HELPING OTHERS

Another surefire way to ease loneliness is helping others—especially others who are lonely. Volunteering for Meals on Wheels or other organizations that support isolated seniors is one idea. Becoming a Big Brothers Big Sisters mentor is another. Or maybe you have a neighbor or family member who might also be lonely; doing little things to support them and provide them some companionship can go a long way.

The amazing thing about helping others is that it's almost always a win-win situation. Others are helped, and so are you. According to one study, eighty-two percent of older adults reported that volunteering helped them feel less lonely. That's because lasting friendships are established, and doing good fosters a sense of belonging and purpose. Significantly, helping others also builds that all-important self-esteem we talked about.

Keep in mind that you don't have to do big things to make a big dent in your loneliness. If you can't undertake a substantial volunteer commitment for any reason, that's perfectly fine! Small efforts can yield outsized rewards. Simply offer a little of your time, presence, or talents, and watch what happens.

## BUILDING A SATISFYING SUPER-CIRCLE

We've now stepped through all the concentric circles of connection, starting with you at the center and working your way outward to proximity. We've added in companion animals and helping others. How are you feeling about your super-circle of connection—that overall circle that holds its arms around all the others?

If you're feeling lonely, you may be thinking that it's too much. You can't possibly be expected to build a solid super-circle. Your loneliness and any significant losses that may have contributed to your loneliness might have left you feeling despondent and tired. The natural lethargy of grief as well as possible self-esteem and/or mobility challenges may be sapping your hope.

To rectify your loneliness, you don't need to do everything all at once. You don't need to do everything period. To get started, all you need to do is choose one self-love practice and one building connection practice. You might begin, for example, by doing breathing exercises whenever you feel depressed or anxious and making a point of chatting with a neighbor once a day. Or you could begin to pursue one single interest or hobby outside of your home, which accomplishes both self-love and building connection.

With intention as well as proximity, repetition, and quality time, small self-care and connection-building steps will tend to compound. You will know your super-circle is satisfying to you when your loneliness starts to ease and you feel more at home in your life.

# A FINAL WORD

*"Once you choose hope, anything's possible."*
— Christopher Reeve

I'm sorry you've been feeling lonely. Even though loneliness is a very common human experience, it's still painful. The good news is that there is help, and there is hope.

Hope is an expectation of a good that is yet to be. It is a forward-looking feeling that sees the future as positive. But the secret is that hope can be more than a feeling. It can also be an action and a practice, and I want you to think of it that way.

You can passively wait for hope to drift by, or you can cultivate it. Here's how: Build pursuits, passions, and people into your daily life that make you feel hopeful. In fact, stop right now and spend a minute asking yourself, "What makes me feel hopeful? What or who gives me that buoyant sense that I can feel connected again, that there are activities and relationships to look forward to in life?"

Whatever the answers to those questions are for you, at least one of them belongs on your schedule each and every day. Watching the sun rise, planning to give a gift, scheduling a fun activity for a week from now, signing up to take a class— do something every day that gives you something *else* to look forward to on a future day. In fact, I invite you to put down this book right now and plant a seed of hope. Spend five minutes doing one thing that reminds you that your tomorrows indeed offer happiness and connection.

And if you're having a hard time mustering hope? Then you can borrow it from someone else. I bet you know someone who always seems like a bundle of joy and energy. Talking to that person may lift your spirits. You can also borrow hope by watching an inspirational movie or reading an inspirational book.

I am hopeful about you finding your way through loneliness. In my career, I have worked with many lonely people who have worked to rebuild self-esteem and connection with others. Their lives have been transformed for the better by the concepts and small daily practices we've covered in this book. Yours can be transformed, too. Namaste.

If You're Lonely

# THE LONELY PERSON'S BILL OF RIGHTS

As a precious, singular human being who needs and deserves love and connection, you have certain rights that no one can take away from you. The affirmations in this list will help you find your way through loneliness.

1. **I HAVE THE RIGHT TO BE LONELY.**

   Loneliness is a common challenge in our culture today. It is often caused by the structure of modern life. If I am lonely, it is a normal human response, and it is nothing to be ashamed of.

2. **I HAVE THE RIGHT TO EXPRESS MY LONELINESS.**

   Acknowledging and expressing my feelings, including my loneliness, is good for me. It helps me cope and builds my emotional intelligence.

3. **I HAVE THE RIGHT TO WANT TO EASE MY LONELINESS.**

   Loneliness is bad for me. It hurts me emotionally and spiritually, and it endangers me physically.

### 4. I HAVE THE RIGHT TO BEFRIEND MYSELF.

Good self-esteem and self-care are essential to befriending others. I must befriend myself as part of finding my way through loneliness.

### 5. I HAVE THE RIGHT TO BE VULNERABLE.

By allowing myself to be vulnerable, I am opening myself to connection. Paradoxically, vulnerability is where my power lies.

### 6. I HAVE THE RIGHT TO BE CONNECTED WITH OTHERS.

Humans are social creatures. I need other people in my life in all of the circles of connection. I am deserving of companionship and connection.

### 7. I HAVE THE RIGHT TO WANT AND NEED MEANINGFUL RELATIONSHIPS.

The quality of my relationships matters more than the quantity. If I have relationships with other people that are not fulfilling to me, I have the right to seek out and build different relationships that are fulfilling.

### 8. I HAVE THE RIGHT TO FOCUS ON PROXIMITY, REPETITION, AND QUALITY TIME.

When I want to build better relationships, I can focus on proximity, repetition, and quality time. These tools will help me make stronger connections.

If You're Lonely

9. **I HAVE THE RIGHT TO COUNT COMPANION ANIMALS AMONG MY INTIMATE RELATIONSHIPS.**

Companion animals can provide me with companionship, presence, unconditional love, touch, and a sense of purpose. They can also help connect me with other people.

10. **I HAVE THE RIGHT TO BE INTENTIONAL ABOUT MY QUEST TO BE CONNECTED.**

Building and maintaining meaningful connections with myself and with others takes effort. When I envision my connected future and then work toward it, I am using the power of intention to build the life I want and deserve.

### The Journey Through Grief

REFLECTIONS ON HEALING | SECOND EDITION

This revised, second edition of *The Journey Through Grief* takes Dr. Wolfelt's popular book of reflections and adds space for guided journaling, asking readers thoughtful questions about their unique mourning needs and providing room to write responses.

ISBN 978-1-879651-11-1 • 152 pages • hardcover • $21.95

### First Aid for Broken Hearts

Life is both wonderful and devastating. It graces us with joy, and it breaks our hearts. If your heart is broken, this book is for you. Whether you're struggling with a death, break-up, illness, unwanted life change, or loss of any kind, this book will help you both understand your predicament and figure out what to do about it.

ISBN: 978-1-61722-281-8 • softcover • $9.95

### The Wilderness of Grief

A BEAUTIFUL, HARDCOVER GIFT BOOK VERSION OF
*UNDERSTANDING YOUR GRIEF*

*The Wilderness of Grief* is an excerpted version of *Understanding Your Grief*, making it approachable and appropriate for all mourners. This concise book makes an excellent gift for anyone in mourning. On the book's inside front cover is room for writing an inscription to your grieving friend.

ISBN 978-1-879651-52-4 • 112 pages • hardcover • $15.95

All Dr. Wolfelt's publications can be ordered by mail from:
Companion Press, 3735 Broken Bow Road, Fort Collins, CO 80526
(970) 226-6050 • www.centerforloss.com

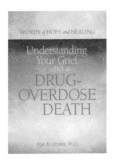

## Understanding Your Grief After a Drug-Overdose Death

In this compassionate guide, Dr. Alan Wolfelt shares the most important lessons he has learned from loved ones who've picked up the pieces in the aftermath of a drug overdose. Readers will learn ideas for coping in the early days of their grief, as well as ways to transcend the stigma associated with overdose deaths. The book also explores common thoughts and feelings, the six needs of mourning, self-care essentials, finding hope, and more.

ISBN: 978-1-61722-285-6 • softcover • $9.95

## Too Much Loss: Coping with Grief Overload

Grief overload is what you feel when you experience too many significant losses all at once, in a relatively short period of time, or cumulatively. Our minds and hearts have enough trouble coping with a single loss, so when the losses pile up, the grief often seems especially chaotic and defeating. The good news is that through intentional, active mourning, you can and will find your way back to hope and healing. This compassionate guide will show you how.

ISBN: 978-1-61722-287-0 • softcover • $9.95

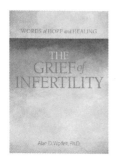

### The Grief of Infertility

When you want to have a baby but are struggling with fertility challenges, it's normal to experience a range and mixture of ever-changing feelings. These feelings are a natural and necessary form of grief. Whether you continue to hope to give birth or you've stopped pursuing pregnancy, this compassionate guide will help you affirm and express your feelings about infertility.

By giving authentic attention to your grief, you will be helping yourself cope with your emotions as well as learn how to actively mourn and live fully and joyfully at the same time. This compassionate guide will show you how. Tips for both women and men are included.

ISBN: 978-1-61722-291-7 • softcover • $9.95

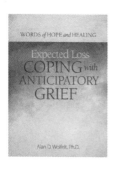

### Expected Loss: Coping with Anticipatory Grief

We don't only experience grief after a loss—we often experience it before. If someone we love is seriously ill, or if we're concerned about upcoming hardships of any kind, we naturally begin to grieve right now. This process of anticipatory grief is normal, but it can also be confusing and painful. This compassionate guide will help you understand and befriend your grief as well as find effective ways to express it as you live your daily life.

ISBN: 978-1-61722-295-5 • softcover • $9.95

All Dr. Wolfelt's publications can be ordered by mail from:
Companion Press, 3735 Broken Bow Road, Fort Collins, CO 80526
(970) 226-6050 • www.centerforloss.com

## Nature Heals: Reconciling Your Grief Through Engaging with the Natural World

When we're grieving, we need relief from our pain. Today we often turn to technology for distraction when what we really need is the opposite: generous doses of nature. Studies show that time spent outdoors lowers blood pressure, eases depression and anxiety, bolsters the immune system, lessens stress, and even makes us more compassionate. This guide to the tonic of nature explores why engaging with the natural world is so effective at helping reconcile grief. It also offers suggestions for bringing short bursts of nature time (indoors and outdoors) into your everyday life as well as tips for actively mourning in nature. This book is your shortcut to hope and healing…the natural way.

978-1-61722-301-3 • softcover • $9.95

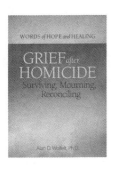

## Grief After Homicide: Surviving, Mourning, Reconciling

Homicide creates a grief like no other. If someone you love died by homicide, your grief is naturally traumatic and complicated. Not only might your grief journey be intertwined with painful criminal justice proceedings, you may also struggle with understandably intense rage, regret, and despair. It's natural for homicide survivors to focus on the particular circumstances of the death as well. Whether your loved one's death was caused by murder or manslaughter, this compassionate guide will help you understand and cope with your difficult grief. It offers suggestions for reconciling yourself to the death on your own terms and finding healing ways for you and your family to mourn. After a homicide death, there is help for those left behind, and there is hope. This book will help see you through.

978-1-61722-303-7 • Softcover • $9.95

All Dr. Wolfelt's publications can be ordered by mail from:
Companion Press, 3735 Broken Bow Road, Fort Collins, CO 80526
(970) 226-6050 • www.centerforloss.com

### Sympathy and Condolences:
### What to Say and Write to Convey Your
### Support After a Loss

When someone you care about has suffered the death of a loved one or another significant loss, you want to let them know you care. But it can be hard to know what to say to them or to write in a sympathy note. This handy book offers tips for how to talk or write to a grieving person to convey your genuine concern and support. What to say, what not to say, sympathy card etiquette, how to keep in touch, and more are covered in this concise guide written by one of the world's most beloved grief counselors. You'll turn to it again and again, not only after a death but during times of divorce or break-ups, serious illness, loss of a pet, job change or loss, traumatic life events, major life transitions that are both happy and sad, and more.

**978-1-61722-305-1 • $9.95 • softcover**

All Dr. Wolfelt's publications can be ordered by mail from:
Companion Press, 3735 Broken Bow Road, Fort Collins, CO 80526
(970) 226-6050 • www.centerforloss.com

**NOTES:**

**NOTES:**

# ABOUT THE AUTHOR

Alan D. Wolfelt, Ph.D., is a respected author and educator on the topics of companioning others and healing in grief. He serves as Director of the Center for Loss and Life Transition and is on the faculty at the University of Colorado Medical

 School's Department of Family Medicine. Dr. Wolfelt has written many bestselling books on healing in grief, including *Understanding Your Grief, Healing Your Grieving Heart*, and *The Mourner's Book of Hope*. Visit www.centerforloss.com to learn more about grief and loss and to order Dr. Wolfelt's books.